Landslides

Jim and Ronda Redmond

Raintree

Nature on the Rampage

www.raintreepublishers.co.uk

Visit our website to find out more information about **Raintree** books.

To order:
- ☎ Phone 44 (0) 1865 888112
- 🗎 Send a fax to 44 (0) 1865 314091
- 💻 Visit the Raintree Bookshop at www.raintreepublishers.co.uk to browse our catalogue and order online.

First published in Great Britain by Raintree Publishers, Halley Court, Jordan Hill, Oxford, OX2 8EJ, part of Harcourt Education.
Raintree is a registered trademark of Harcourt Education Ltd.

Consultants: Lynn Highland, United States Geological Society, National Landslide Information Center; Maria Kent Rowell, Sebastopol, California; David Larwa, Educational Training Services, Brighton, Michigan

Originated by Dot Gradations
Printed and bound in China by South China Printing Company

ISBN 1 844 21219 X
07 06 05 04 03
10 9 8 7 6 5 4 3 2 1

British Library Cataloguing in Publication Data
Redmond, Jim
Landslides. - (Nature on the Rampage)
I.Title II.Redmond, Ronda
551.3'07
A full catalogue for this book is available from the British Library

Acknowledgements
The publishers would like to thank the following for permission to reproduce photographs: Corbis/Chris Rainier, p. **8**; AFP, p. **26**; NOAA, pp. **1, 4, 7, 12, 20, 24**. Root Resources/Doug Sherman, pp. **17, 29**; Unicorn Stock Photos/A Ramey, p. **23**.

Cover photograph by Reuters

Contents

Some landslides sweep cars off roads. They can also cause great damage to roads.

When the Earth slides

Wherever there are hills or mountains, large amounts of rock and soil can move downwards. This is called mass wasting. Mass wasting is the natural transfer of rock or soil downhill. Rocks, earth or mud speed down a slope during a **landslide**. Snow and ice race down hill during an avalanche. Most countries in Europe have landslides or avalanches. They are most common around mountains.

We do not know the exact number of landslides and avalanches that happen each year. They often occur far away from people. Scientists think that almost 500,000 landslides and 1 million avalanches sweep down mountains every year.

Landslides

Many landslides form during the rainy season or when snow melts in spring. When soil and rock is no longer able to hold together on a hillside or mountainside, **gravity** makes the earth slide downwards. Gravity is a force that pulls things towards the centre of huge objects, including our planet and stops them from floating away into space. There are many different ways earth can move down slopes, including **debris flows**, rock slides and falls, flows, **slumps** and **creeps**.

Debris flows, or lahars, are among the fastest and most powerful kinds of landslide. Debris flows are often caused when a volcano erupts. They are made of water and volcanic debris, such as mud, ash and rock. They often come without any warning, so people have little time to move to safety.

A rock slide is a landslide made up of falling rocks. Mud and wet clay form more liquid-like flows. Slumps and creeps are slower and take less land with them. A slump happens when a section of a hillside moves down a short distance. It stops where the soil and rock pile up. A creep happens over a large area of land.

This hillside has been damaged by a creep.

Slumps and creeps can move as slowly as 1.5 centimetres each year. Over time, slumps and creeps can damage buildings, roads, fences and railway tracks. Cracks and bulges in the ground, leaning lamp posts or trees and sticking doors or windows are all signs of creep landslides.

▲ This avalanche is sweeping down a
mountain in the Swiss Alps.

Avalanches

Avalanches usually happen after winter
snowstorms and in the spring. They happen most
in January, February and March.

Layers of snow can create different types of
avalanche. Every time snow falls, it creates a
new layer. A single mountainside can have

Rescuers use dogs to find people who have been buried by avalanches. Dogs can find scents even if they are covered by many metres of snow. A Saint Bernard dog called Barry once found 40 people buried by avalanches.

many layers of snow. All the layers together are called a **snowpack**.

Two common types of avalanche are **sluff** avalanches and **slab** avalanches. Sluff avalanches are made up of the top layer of loose snow. These avalanches happen most often after a snowstorm when the new layer of light snow slides down a mountain. They usually form a triangle-shape as they spread.

Slab avalanches are the most powerful and deadly of avalanches. All the layers of a snowpack can fall at once during a slab avalanche. Large ones carry up to 1 million tonnes of snow and ice down a mountain. Within seconds, the avalanche races along at speeds of up to 160 kilometres (100 miles) per hour. Strong, dangerous winds build up ahead of the fall.

Path of an avalanche

The route an avalanche takes as it moves down a mountain or hill is called its path. Each avalanche has a unique path. Some paths are wide, while others are narrow. Some run straight, while others zigzag down the mountain.

All avalanche paths are made up of three parts. These are the starting zone, the track and the runout zone. The avalanche begins at the starting zone. This place is usually high on a mountain or hill where a great deal of snow falls. As the snow piles higher, it gets heavier and heavier until it slides.

The track is the path an avalanche takes downhill. Avalanches move fast down the **steep** track. They often tear down all trees and plants in their way.

The runout zone is the end of the avalanche path. The avalanche slows down and stops in the runout zone, leaving all of its ice, snow and rocks there.

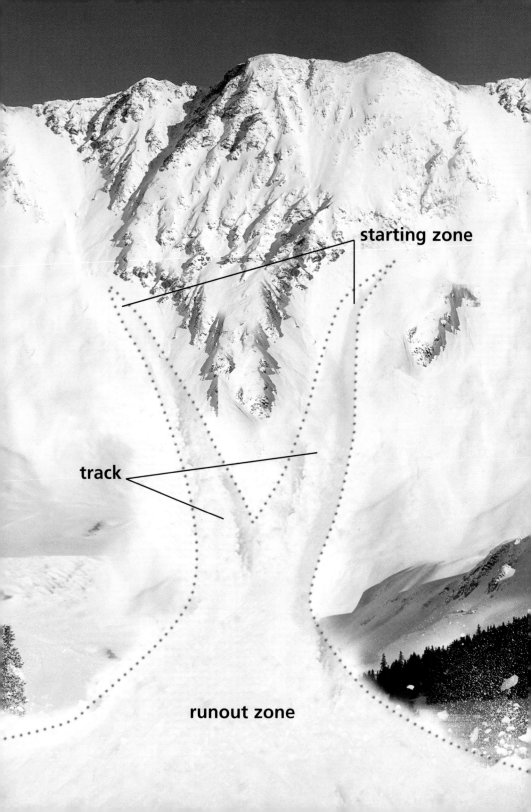

starting zone

track

runout zone

▲ A mudslide has buried part of this
house in mud.

What landslides and avalanches do

Landslides and avalanches tear trees out by the
roots, crush houses and move cars and huge
rocks. When these slides stop, they may bury
whole towns under tonnes of earth, mud or
snow. Many people and animals are also swept
away or buried. It is hard for rescuers to reach

people trapped by these slides. The slides often block roads. They may cause whole sections of road to slide downhill.

People caught in avalanches face dangers. They can crash into trees and rocks as they fall downhill. If they live through the fall, they can be buried and suffocate. Suffocate means to run out of air to breathe.

Even people who are rescued can still die from **hypothermia**. Hypothermia occurs when the body's temperature falls too far below normal. If they do not get help fast enough, they will freeze to death. Only one out of ten people who are caught in an avalanche survives.

Landslides can flow into rivers. When this happens, the landslide blocks the river and stops water from flowing past it. The water might build up behind the landslide until it breaks the river banks and floods the area around it.

As slides fall, they leave **scars**, or bare paths. The snow and earth in these places are likely to fall again.

Snow falls and covers a slope in layers. Each layer may have different properties, for example some will be hard and others soft.

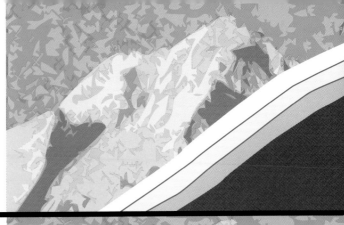

Melting and refreezing during the winter causes older layers to get hard and slippery. Cracks may appear in the top layer.

Movement, noise or gravity can make the top layers break free, sending snow down a slope at up to 160 km/h (100 mph).

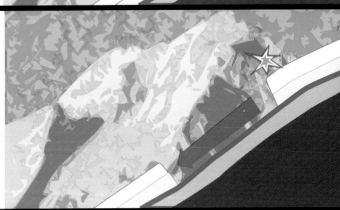

 This diagram shows what can cause an avalanche.

What causes slides?

People sometimes build houses on hillsides. This can cause landslides. They pack the earth lower on the hill, so it will hold the weight of the house. Sometimes they also build stone or cement walls to help hold the hill in place. If all of this is not done correctly, landslides can happen.

People also cause landslides when they cut down too many trees. Without tree roots to help hold rocks and soil in place, landslides can easily happen.

Skiers can cause avalanches by skiing on snow that is **unstable**, or loose. The snow may seem fine on top, but there could be weak snow under the top layer.

Natural causes of landslides

Landslides are more likely to happen on steep hills and mountains. The taller the hill or mountain, the harder it is for trees and plants to hold things in place.

Landslides are common in certain types of soil. Sometimes layers of loose gravel or clay are under the topsoil. These layers may become slippery and cause a landslide.

Earthquakes are another cause of landslides. When earthquakes happen, they break up the ground. This can cause big chunks of earth to fall down the hill. Earthquakes can also loosen large pieces of rock and boulders.

Weather can also cause landslides. When a lot of rain falls in a short time, the earth turns into mud and becomes heavy. Sometimes tree and plant roots are not enough to hold the mud in place, and a **mudslide** forms.

Rock slides often happen when the weather turns from cold to warm. In the winter, water freezes around rocks and in rock cracks. When water freezes, it **expands**, or gets larger. The ice in some cracks grows big enough to split the rocks. In the spring, when the water

▲ **A rock slide has buried this house.**

melts, chunks of rock can break off and fall
down a hill.

Floods can also cause landslides. During floods,
rivers become wider. A river may wash away the
plants and soil at the bottom of a hill. Without
rocks, soil and plants at the bottom, chunks of the
hilltop will fall and cause a slide.

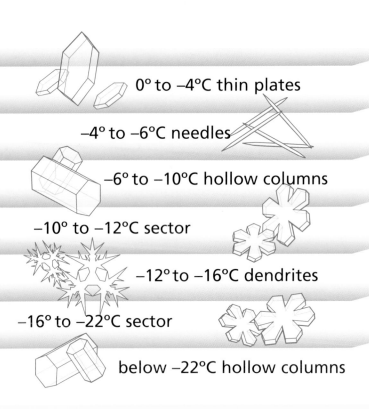

0° to –4°C thin plates

–4° to –6°C needles

–6° to –10°C hollow columns

–10° to –12°C sector

–12° to –16°C dendrites

–16° to –22°C sector

below –22°C hollow columns

▲ **This diagram shows shapes of ice crystals and the temperatures at which they form.**

What causes avalanches?

To understand how an avalanche starts, you must know about different types of snow. All snow is made of tiny ice crystals. These crystals are different shapes depending on the type of snow. Some ice-crystal shapes help snow stick together better. Heavy snow holds together well.

Light snow does not stick to other kinds of snow well. Because of this, light snow slides more easily than other snow.

Layers of light and heavy snow often cause avalanches. For example, avalanches may happen when heavy snow falls on top of light snow or light snow falls on heavy snow.

Temperature changes also cause avalanches. Warmer and cooler temperatures can make the ice crystals change shape. Some layers of snow then become unstable because they do not stick to each other. When a top layer of snow slips off a bottom layer, it creates a sluff avalanche.

Winter storms with heavy snowfalls can cause avalanches. The weight of new snow may make old snow break away from the mountainside and slide downhill.

Wind is a common cause of avalanches. The wind blows loose snow from one part of the mountain and places it on another part. Over time, the snow collects until it becomes too heavy and starts an avalanche.

A landslide has left this scar through the forest.

Slides in history

Slides have happened throughout the Earth's history. We know that people told stories called legends to explain these natural events.

People who lived around mountains often told stories about gnomes. In the legends, gnomes were tiny people who lived inside the mountains. Gnomes made jewellery out of gold and special stones. When they were angry, they did things to upset people, such as throwing rocks down the mountains. People believed these rocks started slides.

In Greenland, stories about gnomes were a little different. They were still said to start avalanches, but these fairytale creatures rode on top of the avalanches as they slid downhill.

California

The state of California in the USA has a history of deadly landslides. These slides happen for many reasons.

There are many hills in California. Earthquakes and heavy rainfalls make the soil and rocks on hillsides ready to slide. Since people build houses in the hills, they may be weakened even more. Hills in California have underlying layers of clay and gravel soil. Top layers of soil slip off the lower layers, or the clay layers can slip off each other, causing slides.

In January 1969, heavy rain fell in coastal areas of California for nine days in a row. During that time, 25 centimetres of rain fell. Mudslides began to fall in the hills of San Gabriel and Santa Monica, near the city of Los Angeles. Rivers of mud ran down the hills and washed away houses and cars.

At the same time, a large river called Santiago Creek filled with water from the rainstorms and mud from the mudslides. People who lived nearby tried to build a wall to keep the river from flooding the city, but this did not work.

▲ A landslide made these houses in California slide down the hill.

Finally, the US Marines used helicopters to pick up cars that were smashed by the mudslides. They built a wall by stacking the cars along the river. This wall stopped the flood from reaching the city.

Scientists study past slides like this one to predict where future landslides may happen.

Studying slides

Many **geologists** study landslides and avalanches. A geologist is a scientist who studies the structure and composition of the Earth. They study the causes of slides and try to find ways to work out when and where slides might happen in future. They also study what kinds of weather might start slides in a certain area.

Scientists learn a great deal by studying landslides and avalanches from the past. They look at things that happened before the slides to discover what may have caused them. They also keep track of changes people make to slopes of mountains and hills. This information helps them to understand slides better.

▲ This scientist is studying the layers of a snowpack to see if they are unstable.

Scientific instruments

Most information about slides comes from geologists' field work. Geologists travel to places where slides happen. They take soil samples and study the kind of earth or snow. They also use maps and computers to make models of places where landslides could happen. They measure the amount of rain or snow that falls and enter it into the computer. The computer then shows them what kind of slide may form and where it would flow. Scientists use the computer to work out what is likely to happen if changes are made to a slope.

Scientists study the temperature of snow layers on a hill or mountain to predict avalanches. To predict is to make an educated guess about when something is likely to happen. Scientists put special thermometers in places where avalanches often happen. The thermometers connect to computers. Scientists use their computers to watch for temperatures that could cause avalanches.

Scientists also dig deep holes in the snow. They study the layers of snow to see how well they are sticking together. They look to see if slipping snow layers are making the snowpack unstable. Sometimes scientists cause little avalanches to see how well the layers stick together.

Preventing avalanches and landslides

Scientists cannot stop every slide from happening, but they do have some ways to control them. People can look at maps to see where slides happen. They can use wire and cement to build big walls or fences in places where landslides and avalanches often happen. These walls hold some of the slide and keep it from falling further down. Stopping some of the slide also helps to slow it down.

People also try to guide landslides away from towns. They dig large pits in the path of slides. The pits stop some of the slide and slow down the fall.

Scientists can prevent deadly avalanches by starting small ones when there is no one there. Today, people fire small explosives into places where they think avalanches will happen. This triggers, or starts, an avalanche. Once the avalanche has stopped, the area is safe for people to walk or ski on once again.

Today, scientists know more about landslides and avalanches than ever before. Scientists can tell how likely it is that slides will form in certain areas. They can warn people who live there.

▲ **People built this wire fence to help hold rocks in place and prevent a landslide.**

The Scottish Avalanche Information Service has joined with the geography department of Edinburgh University to develop an avalanche warning system. It is used for climbers and skiers in the Scottish Highlands. Scientists keep close track of conditions in the mountains.

In Lyme Regis, on the south coast of England, scientists have installed instruments that monitor ground movements and water levels. They study the information to discover if a landslide is likely. They have set up a landslide warning system.

Glossary

creep slow-moving landslide

debris flow landslide containing water and volcanic debris such as mud, ash and rock

expand to get larger

geologist scientist who studies rocks, soils and earth forms

gravity force that pulls objects towards the centre of our planet

hypothermia lower-than-normal body temperature

landslide mass of earth that slides downhill

mudslide landslide made mostly of mud

scar permanent mark from damage

slab avalanche made up of many layers of snow

sluff avalanche made up of the top layer of loose snow

slump slow-moving piece of hillside that falls a short distance

snowpack all the layers of snow on a mountainside

steep having a sharp rise or slope

unstable not fixed or firm

Addresses and Internet sites

British Geological Survey Headquarters
Kingsley Dunham Centre
Keyworth
Nottingham, NG12 5GG

Scotland Avalanche Information Centre
www.sais.gov.uk/about_avalanches

**United States Geological Survey Geologic
Hazards – Landslides**
www.landslides.usgs.gov/

GeoResources
www.georesources.co.uk

Avalanche Education Center
www.csac.org

Index